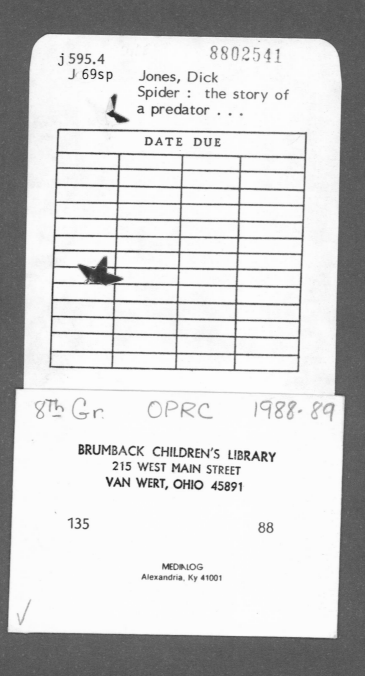

SPIDER

The story of a predator and its prey

written and photographed by
Dick Jones

Facts On File Publications
New York, New York ● Bicester, England

The publishers would like to thank the following organisations and individuals for their permission to reproduce the additional photographs in this book:

Anthony Bannister/NHPA 45 below left; James Carmichael Jnr/NHPA 28; Stephen Dalton/NHPA 45 top; Adrian Davies/ Bruce Coleman Ltd 46/47; Mary Evans Picture Library 6, 8 (©Barbara Edwards); Sonia Halliday and Laura Lushington 7 left; K.G. Preston-Mafham/Premaphotos Wildlife 16; John Shaw/ Bruce Coleman Ltd 26

Orb web artwork by Richard Lewington/The Garden Studio
All other line drawings by Christopher Shields

Illustration right: a doomed grasshopper has fallen foul of *Agelena labyrinthica's* large and complex sheet web

First published in the United States of America by
Facts On File, Inc.,
460 Park Avenue South, New York, NY 10016

First published in Great Britain by
Orbis Book Publishing Corporation Limited
A BPCC plc company

86-45542
ISBN 0–8160–1587–2

Printed in Singapore
10 9 8 7 6 5 4 3 2 1

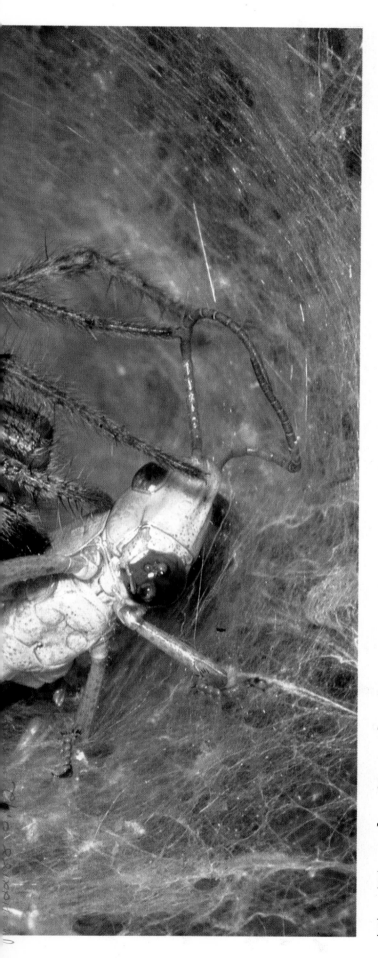

CONTENTS

INTRODUCTION

'The skin of it is so soft, smooth, polished and neat, that she precedes the softest skin'd Mayds, and the daintiest and most beautiful Strumpets, and is so clear that you may almost see your face in her as in a glasse; she hath fingers that the most gallant Virgins desire to have theirs like them, long, slender, round, of exact feeling, that there is no man, nor any creature that can compare with her.'

Dr Thomas Mouffet 1553–1604

In the days when the ancient Greek gods lived on Mount Olympus, a maiden named Arachne, boastful of her skill in weaving, challenged the goddess Athene to a contest to decide which of them was the more accomplished weaver. Athene accepted the challenge and the contestants began work at their looms. When at last they had finished, they turned to look at each other's work. Arachne's tapestry was exceedingly fine, but when she saw the efforts of the goddess, she realised she was beaten. Shattered by the blow of losing the contest after all her boasting, Arachne tried to hang herself. But Athene would not be satisfied by the mere death of her rival, and condemned her to an eternity of spinning and weaving; Arachne was transformed into a spider.

An ancient line
This myth, ingenious though it is, tells us little about the origin of spiders and how they developed their wonderful ability to spin silk. It would seem likely that they evolved from aquatic species

During the mediaeval period, the distinctive markings on A. diadematus (the garden spider) were thought to represent the sign of the cross

Above: *an early 19th century engraving portraying the downfall of Arachne; her arrogance has caused her to be turned into a spider*

nature than we are, and although spiders probably had little direct effect on the lives of our hunting ancestors, their enviable predatory skills were not overlooked.

Weavers of legend

The faint silhouette of a spider surrounded by dead flies adorns the wall of a prehistoric site in a Spanish cave, while on the Nazca Plain in Peru there is a huge outline drawing of a spider amongst the many other mysterious images that can be seen only from the air. On every continent there are spider legends based on close observation of their web-making skills or predatory activities; in many of these, a spider becomes the benefactor of man by teaching him the techniques of basket-making and weaving. Others, however, attributed a villainous role to the spider, in which it took on human form and lured people to their deaths.

Since Roman times spiders have been valued for their supposed power to prevent or cure a bewildering variety of ailments, and they were often worn as a living charm encased in a suitable package and hung around the sufferer's neck. In spite of an admonition at the end of the sixteenth century that these 'foolish toies' were of no use, medical science later intensified its support of the creature and patients were advised to swallow the unfortunate spider, not just wear it; in 1760, one Dr Watson advised that a fever could be cured by 'swallowing a spider gently bruised and wrapped up in a raisin or spread upon bread and butter'.

Spinning and leaping

Meanwhile, in southern Italy, a large wolf spider known as a tarantula (after the port of Taranto) was making its presence felt, and from the fifteenth to the seventeenth centuries a great many peasants were said to have fallen victim to this persistent predator, whose bite resulted in the victim crying, leaping about uncontrollably and launching into a frenetic dance. Whether this performance was a symptom brought on by the poison, or an attempt to purge the body of it is not clear, but in any case the creature lent its name to a lively folk dance in six-eight time, the Tarantella. Confusingly, the term tarantula does not denote a particular spider, but is applied to many large tropical ones, irrespective of their natural affinities.

The writing on the web

A common country belief is that the presence of filmy threads in the grass foretells clear and calm

at the very dawn of life on dry land, emerging from the primeval oceans along with scorpions (like spiders, members of the class Arachnida) and millipedes. Scorpions appear to be descended from the extinct eurypterids (sea scorpions), which resemble giant lobsters, but the ancestry of spiders remains a mystery, like their development in geological times; the fossil record they have left us is maddeningly incomplete since throughout the long ages our world has endured, few spiders have been fossilised, but it is interesting to note that many of these are familiar in their membership of families we recognise now, and in at least one instance they are virtually indistinguishable from the modern species.

The genus *Homo*, to which we belong, emerged in the relatively recent past, about 5 million years ago, but not until 40,000 year ago did modern man appear – 400 million years behind the spiders! Primitive man was more conscious of his place in

Above: *this charmingly painted scene of a spider in peril from a hungry robin is featured on a 15th century glass panel in York Minster*

Above: *our ancestors believed the appearance of fine silvery threads in the grass to be the result of a powerful magic force at work*

weather conditions, but this theory rather puts the cart before the horse; in fact it is only on warm still days, particularly in the autumn, that this material is dispersed.

When warm air currents are rising from the ground, the spiders climb up to elevated positions on blades of grass or twigs and emit long strands of silk from their abdomens. When the lines are long enough to catch this movement of air, the little creatures are borne aloft: this aerial travel is known as 'ballooning'. Very often the spider's journey is quite short, the silken line soon becoming entangled in nearby vegetation, but some spiders have been seen several miles up and others have landed on ships far out at sea.

In particularly good years, millions of tiny spiders are carried through the air each day, and when dusk comes and condensation forms on their lines, they drift slowly down to earth. As soon as they land, still on their lines, they build

their little individual webs of similar material, and the next morning vast tracts of ground are covered in glistening silk. To people in former times, this had the appearance of the goose down commonly seen in late summer when geese were killed and plucked. The time of year – and the substance – became known as 'goose-summer', or gossamer.

Most of the small, black spiders who carry on this aerial dispersal belong to the large *Linyphiidae* family, popularly and collectively known as 'money' spiders. The superstitions associated with finding one of these small creatures on one's person are wide ranging: some believe they are simply bringers of good luck, while others associate them with a gift of new clothes (woven by the spider perhaps) or the acquisition of gold or cash.

Spidermania

Mankind in general has contradictory feelings toward spiders, unwarrantedly attributing good

Above: *since her father, the 16th century physician Thomas Mouffet, believed that spiders had healing properties when eaten, it is not surprising that 'Little Miss Muffet' was distressed at the mere sight of such a creature*

luck to their presence at one moment; in the next, fearing them irrationally. Even in today's aseptic world, when spiders may be feared even more than they were in the past because they are less familiar, most people feel superstitious reluctance to kill one, and will attempt to remove it instead. In the case of some unfortunate individuals, an overpowering and irrational terror of spiders — arachnophobia — rules their lives.

This condition is extremely well-known, although it affects very few people. Indeed, research indicates that more people are afraid of snakes than of spiders; the difference is that snakes are seldom in evidence (except on television), while spiders are a common sight, since we provide shelter for them in our homes, and our food attracts the insects they feed on.

Not all spiders are so enamoured of Man that they wish to live with him — a few steps into the countryside will reveal a wealth of delicate and prettily marked species — but it is one of the many ironies about spiders that the largest, hairiest and most evil-looking are found in and around the house. Unfortunately, among the several species of house spider are those with the greatest leg span, and this is often cited as particularly abhorrent, but most domestic pets have longer, hairier legs and in humans, long legs are deemed attractive.

We don't seem to be so alarmed by cobwebs, but when their builders are caught in our living rooms, that is a different matter. This doesn't happen any more often than the spider can help; most live in their webs, where they will remain contentedly if they are catching the odd titbit, and they can go for considerable periods without food or drink. But if they have not caught anything and are getting hungry, they must move to a new and perhaps better site. It is on these excursions that they tend to be seen, although increased sightings in the autumn may be due to movement by males in search of females. So it is either food or sex that drives them out of the security of their webs into a dangerous and often unsympathetic world. These spiders are desperately vulnerable out of their webs, and when caught out in the open, clinging ludicrously to the walls or strolling across the carpet, they have only two options for staying alive: to remain perfectly still and hope they won't be noticed, or to run as fast as their legs will carry them. They are practically blind, and so can just as easily run towards you as away in their efforts to escape. In fact, the poor creature's fear of man is wholly justified, while our horror and distrust of it constitutes a great injustice. The spider not only does not eat our food; it is a major predator of the insects who do, and since no spider has ever been implicated in spreading disease, they are much less dangerous than even a house fly, which scares nobody.

Labels and fables

When we come to discuss the various types of spiders, we find it necessary to employ Latin names to avoid confusion since, like many creatures, spiders often have no common name or numerous local ones. In the eighteenth century, scientists realised that it would be convenient to ensure that everybody used the same name for each animal or plant and the Swedish scientist Linnaeus devised a system using the classical languages of Greek and Latin with which educated people of all nationalities were familiar. Each organism was given two names, a sort of first name (species) and surname (genus), but in the scientific notation, the 'surname' comes first. If, for example, we take the common European house spider, we find that there are three main species: *Tegenaria gigantea*, *T. domestica* and *T. parietina*. (Note that the scientific names are always printed in italics, and that members of the same genus have their 'surname' abbreviated after the first citation.) The use of the one English name 'house spider' is particularly confusing here, since there are three distinct species. To add to this confusion, the number of species known as house spiders starts multiplying as soon as we leave the confines of one country and go to another. In America, only two of the three English *Tegenaria* species are found, along with the further species *Achaearanea tepidariorum* and *Oecobius annulipes*, both of which are very widespread in warm climates, being found in Australian homes too. Because of the constant traffic between different parts of the world spiders are freely exchanged, although as far as we can tell, the majority of these eight-legged jet-setters originate from Europe. They all might be known as 'house' spiders, yet the three genera mentioned above differ greatly from each other in shape, size and web form. In short, there is no universal house spider, although one of the globe-trotting *Tegenarias* might well take the title eventually.

The identification of the genus and species to which a spider, and any other creature, belongs is part of the scheme that scientists have devised to classify all living things. Naturalists recognise that many animals (and plants) have certain characteristics in common and they have used these to place them also in broader groups than the genus/ species we have been looking at. Collections of genera with similar features are known as *families*, and this applies to spiders as much as to other creatures. (We have already seen that money spiders, for example, all belong to the *Linyphiidae* family.) All spiders together form a vast group known as an order, which is divided into three sub-orders that contain the various families. The two most important of these sub-groups are the *Mygalomorphae* and the *Araneomorphae* (the third sub-order – the *Mesothelae* – contains only nine species), and these divisions are based on the way the spiders' fangs move. The mygalomorph's fangs (A) are vertically placed and parallel to each other, so the spider must rear up to attack its victim with a forward, thrusting movement. The fangs of the

araneomorphs (B) however, are placed in a line, facing each other horizontally, and are able to open and close, catching prey between them.

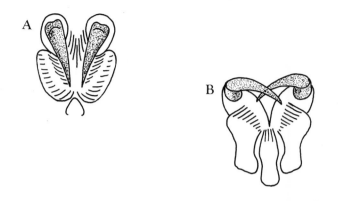

Above: *the wider span of araneomorph spiders' opposed fangs makes it possible for them to overpower large prey*

The *Mygalomorphae* take their name from the Greek words for 'like a field-mouse' from a fancied resemblance to that animal. Some large and imposing species of this group (most commonly the southern American *Brachypelma smithi* or, more colourfully, Mexican Red Knee), are sold in pet shops under the names of 'bird-eating spiders' or 'tarantulas'. Since they mostly eat insects and the name *Tarantula* applies to other sorts of spider as we have seen, neither of the common names is really correct and the term mygalomorph, though not exactly descriptive, is at least universally understood to refer to the same group of spiders.

The *Araneomorphae* are the so-called 'true spiders' and included in this group are the spiders known popularly as the orb web weavers. Whilst they share many physical characteristics, not all of them actually weave webs, so we can see that this common name is inadequate too, whereas the scientific name of the group – *Araneidae* – labels these animals with complete accuracy.

It is easy to see from these examples how misleading the use of popular names in natural history can be, and in fact there is such an enormous number of spider species that most do not even have common names and can only be identified by the scientific terms. This huge range of species is matched by the fascinating variations in behaviour that spiders exhibit and that become obvious on closer examination – as you will see when you read of their exploits in the following pages.

FORM
AND
FUNCTION

'To praise the spider as I ought, I shall first set before you the riches of its body, then of its fortune, lastly of its minde.'

Thomas Mouffet in *Theatrum Insectorum*, 1634

Spiders are not insects – on the contrary they are one of the most important predators of these creatures, which include some of Man's most dangerous adversaries. Spiders are measured by the length of their bodies; the spread of their legs is excluded although it is this that makes them appear much bigger than they really are. The smallest adult spider known is only half a millimetre long, but most spiders measure between 5 and 10mm and the European house spider, despite some descriptions I have heard, is a mere 18mm in body length. In reality, the largest spider known is the hairy South American mygalomorph *Theraphosa leblondii*, a monster with a body 90mm long and a leg span of 280mm – sufficient to cover a dinner plate!

Lethal liquids
Unlike most creatures familiar to us, which must swallow their food and digest it internally, spiders are incapable of swallowing solid particles and consequently have small and inconspicuous

Typical of the jumping spiders, Aelurillus cervinus has large, forward-directed eyes that give clear focus and accurate colour vision

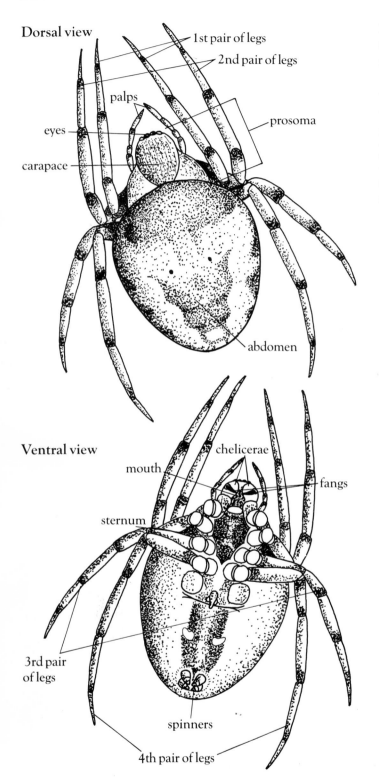

Dorsal view

1st pair of legs
2nd pair of legs
palps
prosoma
eyes
carapace
abdomen

Ventral view

chelicerae
mouth
fangs
sternum
3rd pair of legs
spinners
4th pair of legs

This highly stylised drawing sets out the anatomy of a spider. While the posterior section, the abdomen, is soft, the front portion, the prosoma, is protected by two horny plates, the carapace on top and the sternum underneath. Digestion, circulation, respiration, reproduction and silk production are carried on from the abdomen; locomotion and feeding from the prosoma

mouth parts. The prey is first held in the spider's *chelicerae* (jaws) and punctured by the fangs, which inject a poison.

The chemical composition of spider venom varies considerably from species to species; in a very few kinds there is no poison at all. The infamous black widow spider is armed with a poison that can be lethal or merely unpleasant to human beings, depending on their age, health and size, but out of thirty or forty thousand species of spider only about twenty are dangerous to man.

Once the poison has been injected into the prey, digestive liquids are released over it. When these have liquefied the softer parts of the prey, the resulting 'soup' is ingested by means of the sucking stomach. Some spiders have the base of the chelicerae furnished with teeth that enable them to crush their prey into an unrecognizable mess, but those spiders without these teeth leave their meals in a perfect state of preservation, except, of course, that they are empty husks. Some spiders cannot open their chelicerae very wide, and even with their normal prey, which is small, they can only bite it on an appendage, such as a leg or a wing.

The spider's abdomen is the equivalent of the mammal's trunk, containing the heart, lungs and intestinal tract. In addition, at the posterior end are the characteristic organs of spiders, the three pairs of spinners. The abdomen is covered, like the joints of the limbs, in a soft and elastic cuticle, which in a starved spider can be quite wrinkled, but which after drinking or feeding becomes bloated. Spiders have a low metabolic rate that enables them to go without food for long periods if necessary. Some species of *Steatoda*, for example, are extraordinary survivors: John Blackwell, the famous British arachnologist, kept a *Steatoda bipunctata* in 'a phial which was closely corked and locked up in a book-case . . . from the 15th of October 1829 to the 30th of April 1831, when it died'. This spider endured a fast of eighteen and a half months, and I myself have kept an individual of the same species in a small tube with a completely airtight polythene stopper and an internal volume of about 4cc. After a year I released the spider, none the worse for its deprivations, into my garden. It had survived without food or water and with only about two thimblefuls of air during its confinement.

The hunter and its prey

This ability to survive fasts and the rapacious manner in which spiders attack prey, especially

if they are very hungry, tells us something about their hunting prowess: however clever they may appear in catching, for example, flies, spiders are in fact very inefficient predators. The web weavers do not actively catch their prey – the prey catches itself, rather like a fish caught in a net. Hunting spiders, particularly the nocturnal kinds, do little *real* hunting: if luck permits them to come within striking distance of a potential prey, their senses will inform them of its whereabouts and they will pounce. If they wander all night without coming close to anything tasty then there are plenty more nights in which to have a meal, but the spider that cannot grasp the opportunity to feed when it *does* present itself will not last very long – it will either die of starvation or gradually become weakened and fall prey to one of its fellows or a predatory insect.

Orb-weaving spiders must be similarly speedy in reaching their prey for the web will not hold powerful, struggling insects indefinitely. There is, however, one group of spiders that have no need to hurry in coming to grips with their prey, and do not fear even pompilid wasps, the mortal enemies of most spiders – this group is known as the *cribellates*. Cribellate spiders have an additional

Above: *some spiders like this* Steatoda bipunctata *can survive for over a year between meals, and even shorter-lived ones endure extraordinary fasts; a small wolf spider with a life span of under a year can go 200 days without food*

Above: *the cribellate spider* Amaurobius similis *has on its rear legs a row of bristles covered with tiny cuticular teeth that comb out the silk. Because of its fine structure, cribellate silk can snare any insect unlucky enough to come into contact with it*

Above: *each jumping species has a unique pattern of facial hair, which is often more pronounced in the male, as with* Evarcha arcuata

spinning organ (the cribellum) from which very fine silk can issue, and whereas the threads of ecribellate species (those without the cribellum) are about 1μm in diameter (one twenty-five thousandth of an inch), the cribellate thread is at least a hundred times finer and therefore more efficient in entangling prey.

Close families

Because all spiders are predatory and will readily prey on other spiders as well as insects, it is surprising to find that one or two weaving species live socially, at least for a time. Newly-hatched spiderlings living in very close proximity to each other for various lengths of time are usually at a stage where the predatory habit has not yet developed, and are still subsisting on the remains of the egg yolk within them. A few species feed their young whilst they remain 'at home' so it can

be assumed that they can differentiate between food and family at this early stage. However, once they take up their solitary lives as hunters and weavers, family ties are well and truly broken and they will eat each other.

There are various mechanisms among the hunting spiders that prevent too much cannibalism within the species. Individuals that have grown large hunt in places where larger prey is to be found; the young ones usually occupy a different stratum of the habitat (often nearer the ground), where they are removed from the attentions of the larger spiders, and yet where they can find the small prey they can easily deal with.

Adult males have a shorter span of life than females. This is long enough for them to mate but most males die before the female lays her eggs, removing any competition between them for food and allowing the females to fatten up and so lay more eggs. Although there is a widely-held belief that, with spiders, the wedding breakfast consists of the groom (and certainly it is not unknown for the female to devour her mate) more often the

happy couple enjoy a relationship not found in many of the so-called higher animals.

In a number of species, including the European house spider, the male co-exists quite peacefully with his mate; a week or two after mating, he becomes gradually more lethargic and, his role in life completed, dies – then the female may scavenge on his remains. This may sound gruesome to us, but for the female spider it would be a waste of protein to let the corpse go uneaten – a simple case of waste not, want not.

Lenses and other senses

Most spiders have eight eyes, but some have six, four, or even one (an oddity found in the jungles of Panama). One Hawaiian species (*Adelocosa anops*), of a genus normally remarkable for the large size of the eyes, has no eyes at all and as a result has been given a comically contradictory common name – no-eyed, big-eyed wolf spider. Most of the day-active hunting spiders have reasonably good vision, at least at close quarters, and one orb-weaving spider, *Dinopis*, has eyes that are so big

Above: *the body of a spider is covered in hairs; some are short and fine while others, like those on this* Avicularia, *give a furry effect*

they pass more light to the retina than in any other animal, enabling it to detect movement even at night. It may seem perverse, however, that the majority of eight-eyed species appear to be all but blind, perhaps being able to distinguish little more than day from night. But spiders are literally bristling with an array of other sensory devices for the capture of prey and the avoidance of predators, so it is not surprising that some have abandoned sight in favour of their tactile senses.

Spiders have hairs, spines and bristles known collectively as *setae* (singular *seta*) that are often difficult to distinguish from each other. A few spiders have very short, fine setae and appear almost hairless, but others are quite furry with hairs of different colours making up a pattern. All the setae have sensory functions and are connected to the animal's brain, giving information on the proximity and nature of its prey.

Above: *their highly articulated limbs make spiders well-constructed to manipulate prey. This hapless moth is being devoured by a crab spider*

Spiders are well known for their long hairy legs, and it is on these that the most sensitive setae are to be found. At the ends of the legs and *palps* (leg-like appendages) there are numerous hairs that have hollow tips and are sensitive to chemical substances, endowing the animal with what has been called a 'touch-taste' sense. An orb web spider may have more than a thousand of these chemo-sensitive hairs concentrated on the last segment of each leg. As soon as the prey is touched it can be assessed as being palatable or not; at the same time its size can be estimated – most hunting spiders will not tackle prey larger than themselves, although there are some notable exceptions to this: the male crab spider *Thomisus* is only 3mm long, yet it has even been known to ambush bees.

Spiders also have extremely fine hairs, known as *trichobothria*, set in sockets with a flexible membrane that allows the hairs to waft with the faintest disturbance of the air, such as might be caused by the movement of prey.

Versatile legs
The flexibility of the legs is demonstrated by the ability of the weaving spiders, when knocked out of their webs, to fold their legs into the carapace (head and chest region) forming a protective ball shape. This may well give them some protection from birds, since the spiders can remain motionless for minutes with a less leggy, and therefore less spidery appearance. Looked at under a magnifying lens, such a specimen presents rather a comic sight – eight bright little eyes peering out through a cage of legs.

The ability of the legs to grasp like human fingers allows the free-living hunting spiders to catch and hold on to their prey. They are aided in this task by having the extremities of the legs furnished below or at the tip with a thick brush of hairs called a *scopula*. The end of each individual hair is split into thousands of filaments that are covered in a thin film of moisture, enabling them to stick to smooth surfaces. The spider's scopulae are very efficient – even some of the largest spiders can walk or hang on a sheet of the smoothest glass. In some families the scopulae are modified to hold on to prey rather than surfaces, but in both cases this brush of hairs allows the spider to retain its prey better once it has been caught.

All spiders have two claws terminating each leg; a few species have a single claw at the end of each palp as well. Unlike hunting spiders, weavers never have scopulae – instead they have, between the others, an additional claw with which they grip the lines of their web. The spiders that get trapped in our baths and hand-basins are always weavers – hunting spiders can easily walk up the slippery sides and continue their wanderings.

Booklungs and heartbeats
Insects breathe through *trachea* – tiny tubes that penetrate into the body and are responsible for the diffusion of oxygen. In addition, spiders are equipped with lungs: mygalomorphs have two pairs, araneomorphs a single pair. They are formed of tiny leaves like the pages of a book and are known as *booklungs*. The breathing system is not very efficient in spiders, particularly in the larger species, which soon become breathless if forced to run very far. Spiders are masters of the fast attack, but whilst they are remarkable in being able to move swiftly after being totally motionless for long periods, they cannot, in general, sustain such activity for more than a few seconds.

The spider's heart is to be found at the front end of the abdomen and it is often marked by a longitudinal patch. This patch, where it exists,

forms part of the pattern on the spider's back. In an exhausted spider, the heart can be seen pulsating by means of the regular motions of the white parts of the pattern. Larger spiders have slower heart beats (50 per minute) than smaller ones (more than 100 per minute) and an active spider can increase its heart rate by a factor of nearly four times over the resting state.

Spiders and man

The large mygalomorphs that feature in film and television as the personification of the deadly animal are chosen mainly because their larger size makes them easier to film. If anything they are less poisonous than their smaller relatives, relying on their size and strength rather than poison. However, some of the mygalomorphs have, on their abdomens, special hairs they can brush off with their rear legs. If these get inhaled or penetrate the skin, they can have an unpleasant effect like the hairs of nettles. For this reason they are known as *urticating* hairs, from the scientific name of the nettle – *Urtica*.

Spiders are so conditioned to feeding on insects that they are most unlikely to bite us except in self-defence. Many spiders will nip if held in the

Above: *the poison of* Thomisus onustus *is fatal to insects but harmless to man. Here, its bright colouring provides camouflage on a flower*

fingers, but if allowed to walk over our hand they will do just this and are no more likely to bite us than they would attack the ground or vegetation on which they walk. Although the Black Widow spider has been implicated in numerous cases of envenomation in America, I once kept one and found it to be a timid creature. On several occasions it accompanied me to lectures where I demonstrated its ability to pull in its legs and feign death, which it did at the lightest touch. I have also had the European Black Widow walk harmlessly across my hand while I was trying to photograph it in its retreat. Yet in the same circumstances I have been bitten by a *Thomisus* crab spider who was guarding her eggs, and also by a *Chiracanthium* spider emerging from her egg sac. Now, *Thomisus* has a poison that acts swiftly on large bees, and whilst I felt the prick of its fangs, I could see no signs of the bite and felt no effects whatever. Some *Chiracanthium* species are reckoned to be poisonous to man but again I suffered no ill-effects. If only mosquito bites were so innocuous!

SPIDER VAGRANTS

'. . . they toil not neither do they spin'
St Matthew 6:28

Naturalists divide spiders into three broad ecological groups. The first of these, web-builders, live in or near their webs and rely on them to snare their prey passively. The other two, tube dwellers and vagrant hunters, depend on active assault to overwhelm their victims, but while tube dwellers do their hunting from the security of a permanent base, vagrants build only temporary retreats – and some have no permanent home at all.

In the popular imagination, spiders and webs are inseparable, but there are numerous species that make little use of silk to catch their prey – these are the vagrant hunters. Some are active only during the daytime and depend mainly on their keen sight, while others work only at night, groping about in the dark until something they can eat wanders near. Although it might seem extraordinary that a hunting animal should be virtually blind, most of the spiders that hunt at night appear to have lost the use of their eyes in favour of their finely-tuned tactile senses: vibrations caused by potential prey are relayed to them through the

The flies seeking a meal in this bloom are themselves about to become food for the wandering crab spider Diaea dorsata

Above: *well-camouflaged, the central American species* Sicarius rugosus *burrows into the sand to await its prey. Here, a doomed beetle larva has blundered into the buried hunter*

Above: S. thoracica *does not need an accurate aim to shoot its gluey poison, since the liquid spreads widely. The fly is consumed through a tiny puncture, and only a husk is left (top)*

vegetation on which the spiders climb, or picked up through the air by the fine hairs (*trichobothria*) that occur near the extremities of their legs. Once their prey is located, many hunting spiders use highly specialised procedures for disabling and devouring it.

Sticky threads

Although its original habitat is under stones and in deep vegetation in southern Europe, one of the most interesting hunters, the Spitting Spider or *Scytodes thoracica* is now found in houses in the north of the continent as well, and it has even been transported to America and Australia, where it has also become a domestic spider. *Scytodes* has developed a predatory technique not found in any other genus of spider. When prey is sensed at a distance of a couple of centimetres, the spider turns to face it and gives a rapid shudder, firing strong, sticky threads composed of a mixture of poison and glue

that leave its victim rooted to the spot, struggling to escape. *Scytodes* then cautiously steps forward and administers a poisonous bite. The hunter needs the advantage of this immobilisation since its chelicerae are small and parallel, incapable of much lateral movement. The fangs are also quite tiny so the spider is able to bite only a leg or a wing.

These spiders use this special weapon for both attack and defence, and seem to catch most of what comes into range, but a serious drawback is that prey must first chance to approach very closely before the method can be called into use.

Deadly concealment

Because the number and arrangement of their eyes is similar to *Scytodes*, sicariid spiders were once grouped with them by arachnologists but these latter, known as 'six-eyed crab spiders', are quite different in appearance and technique from the Spitting Spider.

Imagine a sandy, tropical location; a luckless insect is making its way across the sand, intent on finding food. Suddenly it is surrounded from below by six knobbly legs, stabbed with poisonous fangs and held fast – *Sicarius rugosus* (the six-eyed crab spider has found its meal for the day. The colour and texture of this spider are very similar to those of the sandy soil; it buries itself just below the surface, forelegs exposed but well camouflaged. Perhaps it can feel the vibrations as its prey approaches, or possibly it reacts rapidly when its victim unwittingly touches it. Sight certainly plays no part, because the spider's eyes are covered with sand along with the rest of its body.

Above: Thomisus onustus *is known for its predation of bees. The spider strikes at the 'neck', avoiding the sting and sending its poison straight to the main nervous system*

Above: Xysticus kochi *sometimes preys on the weevils that threaten plants and stored produce* Overleaf: *a hoverfly falls victim to the crab spider* Misumena vatia *lurking on a seed head*

Also known as crab spiders, the *Thomisidae* family will eat almost any kind of prey, regardless of size. If we can spot this spider waiting for its meal (and this is not always easy since it is shaped and coloured to match the plants it lives among) we notice first that although its eyes are small and widely separated, the spider sees us and extends its heavy front legs. As we get closer, it possibly thinks this is the biggest insect it has ever seen! Closer still and any anticipation it might have had of a large meal turns into the suspicion that we might be a predator, and the spider scuttles off sideways, just like a diminutive crab. Crab spiders are the antithesis of the general image of a hunter, since they tend to be rather stout and slow-witted creatures. They are by no means blind, but their sight is not good and their chelicerae are tiny – so how do they manage to thrive? Their weapons are patience and a poison strong enough to paralyse formidable insects like bees, or strong flyers such as butterflies. In addition, some of the 'crabs' (those known as flower spiders) conceal themselves in the blooms and ambush visiting insects. Not only do these species match the colour of the petals, but many have curious shapes that mimic plant forms and so help to disguise their presence.

Once a large insect is caught, the spider holds it with the first two pairs of legs, which are particularly long and strong. It then administers a bite at the junction of the insect's head and thorax. Once the quick-acting, virulent poison has paralysed the prey, the spider's legs release their hold and it is gripped solely with the fangs.

As with some other hunting spiders, the prey's corpse appears totally unmarked after the 'crab' has finished with it.

Varied diet

Xysticus is a genus of crab spider that has a large number of species scattered around the world.

Above: *the divergent chelicerae and long fangs of* Dysdera crocata *allow it to penetrate the tough dorsal plates of a woodlouse.*

Most of these feature various shades of brown markings, which serve them well since they forage on the ground and among low plants. Unlike their gaudier relatives, *Xysticus* spiders do not come into contact with particularly large, powerful adversaries, but they will eat an astonishing variety of prey, some of which is seldom if ever tackled by other hunting spiders: winged ants, weevils and other small beetles all feature on their menu. Well-armoured prey like these have only one weak spot in their design – the articulations of the legs, where the cuticle is thinner to allow for bending – and this is the precise point where *Xysticus* buries its fangs.

Another spider that has six eyes like *Sicarius* and *Scytodes* is, like the latter, cosmopolitan, and has its origins in the Mediterranean region. This is *Dysdera*, a garden spider, which is one of the few hunting species that catch and eat woodlice. These land crustaceans pull in their many legs and hold themselves down when threatened, and whereas most spiders would be quite incapable of piercing or even gripping their tough dorsal plates, *Dysdera* has such long fangs that they can be pushed under the edge of these plates to lever the woodlouse up. Once the softer underside is accessible, the spider can pierce it with his fangs and inject it with poison. Fortunately for *Dysdera*, the smallness of its appetite and the density of the woodlouse population ensure that it never faces a food shortage.

The flesh-coloured abdomen and reddish carapace of *Dysdera* give it a distinctive and rather unpleasant appearance. It is one spider I would not be happy to handle, since its spreading chelicerae are capable of giving a nasty nip to a human as well as an insect.

Intrepid fighters

Many spiders, including such comparatively aggressive species like *Dysdera crocata*, will avoid encounters with ants, but more interestingly, there are a few spiders who actually live solely or mainly on these aggressive little creatures. Some species of ant-preying spider mimic their prey in behaviour or appearance, although the reasons for this remain a matter of scientific conjecture. One of these is *Callilepis*, a small genus of spider (found in Europe, America, India and Japan) that has

evolved a unique method of dealing with them. When *Callilepis* encounters a potential meal, it adopts a stance geared for a quick lunge, raising its front legs to locate the insect's antennae, and then making a quick bite at their base. The ant is fairly aggressive when it meets the much larger spider, but on being bitten it is even more fierce, so the spider immediately retreats to await the curious event that subsequently takes place. The poison acts first on the antennae, which soon become limp and useless so that in the death throes that follow, the ant turns helplessly in circles, no doubt because of the loss of sensitivity in these organs. Mortally wounded, it cannot run away, and eventually the spider returns, this time to deliver a longer bite. Once the ant is completely paralysed, *Callilepis* grips it in its fangs and carries it away from any other ants, to a spot it has previously covered over with silk for protection. The spider feeds through one or two small bites on the neck and abdomen of the ant, which is left as an empty husk after a couple of hours.

Zodarion, another exclusive ant predator, is found mainly in Europe and North Africa, and the most telling evidence of its presence is the piles of dead ants it leaves beneath stones. These spiders

Above: C. schuszteri *is unusual in eating ants, which often prey on spiders. Ants also contain formic acid, which repels most vagrants*

Above: *the glossy bodies and slender legs of* Zodarion *spiders give them a similar appearance to the ants on which they prey*

have a very similar method of attack to *Callilepis*, although their fatal bite is normally aimed at antennae rather than the body, since they have only small, feeble chelicerae that are joined at the base and so cannot open very far.

It is remarkable that such ill-equipped hunters are not only *capable* of tackling ants (among the most pugnacious of insects) – they actually *specialise* in them.

High jumpers

The *Salticidae* are the largest family of spiders and its members are popularly known as jumping spiders or 'jumpers'. Among arachnologists they are regarded with some affection as they have good eyesight and an engaging curiosity.

On one occasion I was trying to photograph a

Below: *jumping spiders have a remarkably flexible prosoma that enables their eyes to be turned in different directions*

male *Heliophanus* that seemed to have a pressing engagement elsewhere. Hoping to frighten him into a standstill so that I could get my shot, I blocked his path with my free hand. Undeterred, he jumped straight onto it, so I flipped my wrist to propel him back onto the ground. He landed facing away from me, and then turned towards me, his eyes looking me up and down in such a disdainful way that I was really sorry I had been so rough with him!

The salticid eyes can certainly spot a large object like a human at several feet, but smaller fry such as its normal prey must be closer before it is noticed. When the 'jumper' sees a possible meal nearby, it begins to stalk it in a kitten-like way, running a few steps and stopping, its palps working up and down as if in delight at the prospect of a meal. In

vegetation, the spider will leap from twig to leaf to follow its prey, but on a smoother surface the stalking is done in a series of short dashes interspersed with sudden stops. All the time the prey is transfixed by the large eyes, and when it is within range, the spider leaps upon it. If, as frequently happens, the prey is aware of the spider's approach and flies off a split second before the leaping spider reaches it, the spider is left in a professionally embarrassing situation. It does not look around for the missing insect as we might in such circumstances, but carefully wipes its eyes with its palps before moving away.

Salticidae are unique among jumping animals in that they lack a greatly enlarged pair of back legs, yet many are prodigious leapers and one species *Attulus saltator* can span a distance greater than twenty times its own length when it is threatened. All spiders have muscles in their legs, but these can only bend the leg, not stretch it; the jumping spiders accomplish their leaps by means of a hydraulic mechanism that inflates the limbs and causes them to be stretched.

Skillful hunters

The wolf spiders (those of the family *Lycosidae*) are immediately recognisable from the arrangement of

Above: *wolf spiders such as* Alopecosa fabrilis *can reach lengths of 25mm, and have strong enough chelicerae to tackle even very heavily armoured insects such as beetles*

their eyes in three rows on the carapace – four small ones at the front, and two large ones in the middle and back rows respectively. The predatory behaviour of the lycosids is more varied than that of the saltacids: some are fairly similar in making a lunge towards their prey without any preliminary stalking, others hunt from burrows like mygalomorphs do, and yet others make sheet webs. Their eyesight is good, but not quite up to the standard of the jumping spiders, and, in complete contrast to that family, some of the larger species of wolf spider are nocturnal.

In northern Europe they are typified by the genus *Pardosa*, small active spiders that frequent the ground. One species, *Pardosa lugubris*, is particularly numerous in and around woods, and it is often possible to hear them scampering about on the dry, fallen leaves. They do not actively chase their prey, although they are good runners and can make small leaps to speed themselves along the ground. Unlike jumping spiders, which spring from a standing start, 'wolves' incorporate

their leaps into a run; even so, they never jump farther than a few body lengths.

The largest British wolf spider is *Alopecosa fabrilis*, widespread in Europe but occurring in England only on two sandy heaths in the south. The chelicerae of *Alopecosa* are large and powerful, and this spider probably depends more on its strength than on the potency of its poison. Certainly, it can cope easily with large flies and it has a strange method of doing so; once it catches the fly, the spider holds it down with its front legs much like a dog would, while stabbing it quickly with the chelicerae. The spider immediately turns a somersault, landing on its back with the struggling fly held aloft. Removing the fly's feet from the ground and grasping its wings, the spider thus ensures that it has no means of escape and, if necessary, *Alopecosa* can reposition its fangs or make slight adjustments to its grip without any fear of the fly getting away. In less than a second the spider rights itself, its victim held firmly by the chelicerae alone.

The burrow of *Alopecosa fabrilis* consists of a closed cell, thinly walled with silk, just below the surface of the sand. Species of the genus *Arctosa* dig a longer tube, sometimes T or Y-shaped, with a thin silk curtain across the entrance. Some lycosids, like the American genus *Geolycosa*, make burrows as deep as one metre; the Australian 'wolves' have shallower burrows but use their silk to attach small pieces of vegetation around the entrance. Other species build a simple mound at the opening to prevent flood-water from entering; yet others adopt the mygalomorph idea of a front door, thick or thin as the case may be (see Chapter 4). All these burrowing lycosids spend their days below ground and at night either sit at their thresholds waylaying passing insects, or wander nearby, grabbing anything they meet.

Fishing for prey

Also known (inaccurately) as wolf spiders are the *Pisauridae* family. None of these make burrows and all are substantial in size but they are not confined to the ground like true wolf spiders. The Swamp or Fisher Spiders of the genus *Dolomedes* are found near water, although immature individuals of the European species *Dolomedes fimbriatus* can be abundant in the foliage of nearby trees. The

Opposite: *found only in or near damp places,* Dolomedes *spiders will take large prey such as minnows which they attract by vibrating the water with their front legs*

habitat of *Dolomedes* has been severely reduced in England – unfortunately, for this is one of the most impressive of English spiders – the powerfully built body can be up to 22mm long in the female.

Dolomedes spiders use the water's surface like a web to transmit the vibrations of potential prey as they station themselves with their forelegs resting on it and their rear legs hanging on to poolside vegetation. Their usual victims are insects, but on occasion they will actually catch fish. The front legs tap the surface of the water, attracting the attention of an insectivorous fish below, and when it comes up to eat what it supposes to be a drowning fly, it is itself grasped by the spider and paralysed by its poison. These spiders will attack not only fish that are marginally bigger than themselves, but also tadpoles and small frogs. In spite of their audacity in tackling these small vertebrates however, they are timid where humans are concerned and will dive below the surface and stay there for several minutes to avoid us.

Tiny wanderers

Before we leave the hunting spiders we should look at some of the midget members of the *Linyphiidae* family – the Money Spiders, whose ballooning behaviour we examined in Chapter 1. Not all of these make webs; some live in leaf litter or tall vegetation and wander about looking for prey in the same manner as many of their larger relatives. As with most hunting spiders, their prey is never larger than themselves, and springtails (small wingless insects) make up a high proportion of their diet. It is also these abundant creatures that figure prominently on the menu for the earliest stages of the most of the other hunting spiders, all of which begin their careers as spiderlings of two or three millimetres in length. The Money Spiders never get any bigger than this and are no more than one millimetre long when they catch their first meal. There is little competition between them and other hunters though, for there is plenty of prey for all. These midgets, in any case, are mostly hatched in the spring when other species tend to be fully grown. This means that in any particular season the spiders in each stage of their development will be hunting for prey of a different size. Furthermore, Money Spiders stay in action throughout the colder months of the year, so that while most other spiders are tucked away for the winter, the linyphiids have unrestricted access to their own small prey – in the northern hemisphere a number are even active under snow.

TUBE
AND
TENT
DWELLERS

*'Will you walk into my parlour?' said a
spider to a fly;
''Tis the prettiest little parlour that ever you
did spy.'*

Mary Howitt, nineteenth century

Some tube dwellers spin a cylindrical home above
ground, but most hollow their retreat out of the
earth, and some of the most fascinating of these are
the *Ctenizidae* or 'trap-door' spiders. Their behaviour, predatory characteristics and especially the
protective devices they have developed to elude
their enemies, are extremely varied and complex,
but the existence of all ctenizid spiders revolves
around the tube or burrow which, as is the case
with all tube dwellers, provides not only protection, but a place of hiding from which it can strike
out at its prey.

The construction of this burrow, with its silk
lining and hinged door, is therefore a vital and
complicated feat of engineering, and one for which
the spider is ably fitted. The ctenizids have a
smooth and rather glossy appearance, but closer
observation of the chelicerae reveals a rake of
thick, short, spiny setae that are used, with the
fangs, to scratch a tunnel out of the earth. The
industrious builder compresses the dug-out soil
into a pellet, carries it to the entrance, then pushes

*Ctenizidae like this eastern Mediterranean species
have a slow growth rate since they feed only on prey
that comes within reach of their burrows*

Above and top: *because it is weathered and colonised by vegetation exactly like the surrounding soil, the earth door of a* Cteniza *burrow is very difficult to discover*

open the 'door' to fling it out. These remarkable doors are of two types, known respectively as 'cork' and 'wafer'. The cork door is thick and has a bevelled edge that fits the rim of the burrow exactly, whereas the wafer door is thinner, without a bevel, but it is manufactured with the same precision. Both types are composed of soil particles cemented together with saliva and bound up with silk; the spider begins to mould the door at its hinge and gradually extends it until it is the same size as the opening of the tube. The spider then feels around the perimeter of the door to detect any irregularities, and fills these with additional pieces of soil. When this has been completed, the spider pulls the door tightly shut, helping to give it a perfect fit. The door is added to periodically whenever the burrow is enlarged, so that older, more established spiders have larger and thicker doors to their burrows than their juniors, or those in newer dwellings. All of the cork doors are heavy

enough to slam shut with their own weight after the spider disappears back into its burrow after one of its rare excursions, so that even specimens living in captivity are rarely seen. In addition, the burrows are extremely difficult to find when the doors are closed as these match their surroundings in soil type and even have the same sort of moss or other small plants growing on top. If you are interested in the well-being of a particular specimen, one way of ensuring that it is still alive is to prop open the door of its burrow with a small twig: if it is still ajar the following morning, fear the worst! If the spider is alive and well it will have removed the obstruction during the night and regained its privacy.

Defensive tactics

Although these spiders are known as *trap-door* spiders, the door is not part of a trap, since a real trap-door would collapse under the weight of an insect and let it fall to the waiting fangs of the spider beneath. *These* doors on the other hand, open outwards, and are designed, as we have seen, to protect the occupant of the burrow from the outside world. They are the first line of defence against the spider's smaller adversaries, such as scorpions, centipedes, pompilid wasps and some flies, as well as larger ones like birds and mammals. In some species, the lower parts of the third pair of legs are modified into shallow U-shapes and furnished with many small spines at their extremities. When a predator approaches, these legs are held above the spider's body and pressed tightly against the walls of its tubular burrow, while the fangs hold on to the underside of the door, preventing the entry of all but the strongest enemy. Even when a knife blade is inserted, the pressure required to raise the door is considerable; one experiment showed that a spider was able to resist an upward force of 38 times its own weight!

If this fails, a trap-door spider with a simple tube burrow is at the mercy of the intruder, but some species, such as the Australian *Anidiops villosus* have another trick up their sleeves. The burrow is lined, as are most, with a layer of silk adhering to the walls. About half way down the tube is a spot that the spider habitually uses as a midden, breaking the silk at that point and placing the remains of its meals 'under the carpet'; having put its rubbish out of sight, it then re-weaves the silk. Should an enemy penetrate the door, the spider rushes down the burrow and pulls down the silken sleeve it has built up around the midden. This

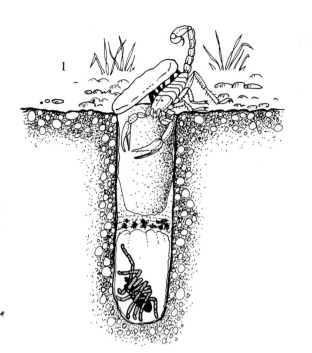

Above: Anidiops villosus *stores its 'leftovers'*
behind a break in the silken lining of its burrow.
When invaded, the spider pulls the loose sleeve
down and releases the debris

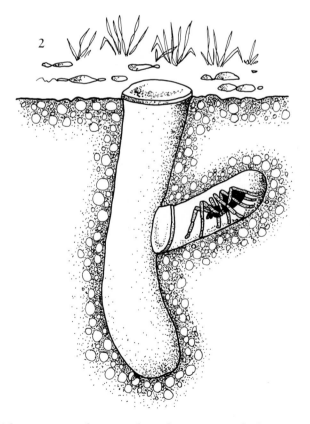

Above: *trap-door spiders from many different*
families protect themselves from predators and flash
floods by building an extra chamber with a second
door into the side of the main burrow

makes a seal across the bottom section of the tube, under which the spider skulks, while the rubbish from out of the walls falls on top (figure 1). When the predator reaches what he believes to be the bottom of the tube and finds only dessicated leftovers, it wanders off to search elsewhere.

One compatriot of *Anidiops*, *Stanwellia nebulosa*, operates a superior form of this disappearing act in which a pellet of compacted earth is stored in the side pocket, making an even more substantial barrier.

Another escape technique is employed by several American and Australian species, which make a side tunnel that itself is furnished with a door. If threatened, the spider rushes below the hanging, inner door and pushes it upward to seal off the upper part of the burrow. If the visitor is not fooled and persists in attempting to open this second door, the spider insinuates itself into the side tunnel while still holding the door up, then suddenly releases it and pulls it against its new hiding place (figure 2). The intruder's feelings of victory soon change to bewilderment and defeat when it finds the lower chamber as empty as the upper. More sophisticated still are the defences of a Venezuelan spider, *Rhytidicolus structor*, which uses no less than three doors to escape its enemies. The outer door leads to an enlarged urn-shaped chamber where the spider waits to pounce or defend, while below this a second door leads to an elongated chamber, which in turn has an inner sanctum half way along, with a third door in it (figure 3).

In spite of the capacity some members of the trap-door family have for complex construction work, others seem to have given up hope of living to tell the tale if they remain in their burrow when invaded by a predatory scorpion or wasp. Their tubes have a simple side tunnel leading up to ground level, camouflaged by a pile of loose earth. If the spider is threatened by a frontal attack it scrambles through the back door and makes its escape through the undergrowth. Even simpler in design is the burrow of another South American spider, *Stothis astuta*, obviously a nervous creature that hedges its bets by making a U-shaped burrow with identical doors at both ends, so that unless it is attacked simultaneously by two predators, it can make a fast exit by either door (figure 4).

One genus of these less ambitious engineers that has developed a particularly astounding method of protective camouflage is *Cyclocosmia*, found in shady ravines in the south-eastern states of the

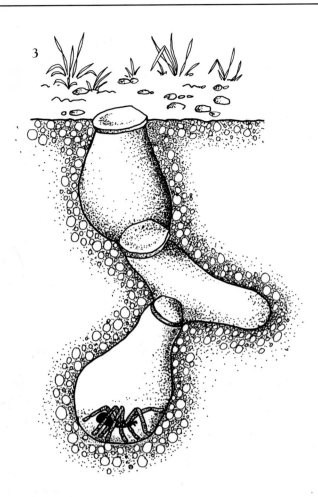

Above: Rhytidicolus structor *from Venezuela provides an even better defence by constructing two further side chambers in its lair. Wily predators that have solved the two-door trick may be fooled by the third door!*

Above: *the U-shaped burrow of the thick-set Caribbean species* Stothis astuta *is almost certainly made this way for defence rather than aggression, but does its construction give two chances to invaders or the fleeing spider?*

USA, in eastern Mexico and in Indochina. Its appearance is particularly distinctive since it has a flattened rear end with a leathery texture and grooves radiating from the centre. The spider makes a plain vertical burrow with a thin, hinged door and a shape that tapers gently downward; when it is invaded, the occupant dives to the bottom, where its broadened posterior fits the diameter of the tube exactly. A predator dashes in to search for the spider, but finds the burrow apparently empty, not realising that the base of the tube is the back end of the spider (figure 5).

From the diversity of their defences, it is obvious that even these spiders, among the largest known, have their share of trials and tribulations. As well as guarding against predators, the 'doors' are a first defence against flash floods and effectively seal the burrow against climatic fluctuations, maintaining a more even temperature and humidity than would be possible out in the open.

Above: Cyclocosmia's *amazing ability to disguise its rear end as the floor of its burrow protects it from most predators. Some parasitic wasps however can not only see through the ruse, but also penetrate the spider's leathery hide*

Above: *the cribellate silk lining of* Filistata insidiatrix's *burrow is combed out into curly strands that will snare any unwary insect*

Above: F. insidiatrix *seems to be sluggish in attacking its prey; it searches for a leg or wing to bite before dragging the insect to its lair*

Hidden dangers

The trap door spider passes its day in the depth of its hole; at night it lurks near the door, ready to catch its prey with a sudden darting movement from underneath it. A few species will wander a very short distance at night, but most will emerge no further than they can reach while clinging with their legs over the entrance so the door is worn like a flat cap shading their gleaming eyes; others are completely hidden, just below the door.

A variation on the hunting technique of the trap-door spiders is practised by *Filistata*, a cribellate genus found in warm climates that, unlike most tube dwellers, is an araneomorph rather than a more primitive mygalomorph. This spider spins distinctive coiled threads that radiate from the burrow and immediately snare any insect foolish enough to come into contact with it.

The ecribellate genus *Segestria*, and the very similar *Ariadna*, also spin strands that radiate from their nesting places, but these serve a different purpose; their long lines of plain silk signal the presence of moving prey to the spider which waits out of sight, deep within its horizotal tube. Unlike other tube-dwellers, and indeed other spiders, *Segestria* and *Ariadna* have three pairs of legs directed forward, only the rear pair pointing backwards. If this arrangement is designed to help

Above: Segestria florentina *preys on flies that sun themselves on the walls near which the spider builds its web. Long radiating lines signal the presence of the moving insect*

them move more quickly out of the tube and along the silken lines, then it is very effective, for they are the fastest of all weaving spiders. The only sure way to discover the precise identity of the owner of one of these distinctive webs is to tickle one of the radiating strands and hope that the occupant of the burrow is fooled into showing itself. Sometimes the spider can be seen cautiously approaching the mouth of the tube but often it comes out as if jet-propelled, probes the vibrating strand, reverses direction without turning and then disappears – all in a fraction of a second. On one occasion, I crouched down to observe the large European *Segestria florentina* near the bottom of a wall. After I had spent a minute or so tickling the web, the spider suddenly advanced with such speed that I was literally bowled over. By the time I had picked myself up it was deep within its tube again, and further fruitless tickling showed that it had got wise to me. These spiders often look remarkably large for the size of the burrow they occupy, but they have no need for space to turn around in as they can run backwards just as fast as forwards.

Family patterns
When they survive the perils of the natural world, trap-door spiders in particular are very long-lived, and a fortunate female might spend twenty years or more living in her hole in the ground. The males mature after several years of this existence, then suddenly vacate their prisons for a brief airing above ground when they search for a female – in good seasons they can be seen in huge numbers. Mating takes place in the female's burrow and in due course she lays eggs; the newly hatched spiderlings spend several months with their mother before wandering a short distance and digging

Above: *the Mediterranean tent builder* Uroctea durandi *is beetle-like in shape and markings. If forcibly ejected from its home, it scuttles to the nearest crevice much like a beetle would*

Inset: *the spider's retreat is commonly found suspended a few millimetres below a large rock. The signal lines are also suspended on silk pylons so vibrations are relayed straight to the spider*

their own burrows. Two Australian species are known to balloon and can travel over considerable distances, but the majority disperse on foot, thus forming closely grouped colonies.

A safe retreat

Related to the tube dwellers are the spiders known as 'tent dwellers'. Their retreats (the design of which would appear to be a modification of those tubular homes that are spun above ground) are convex silken structures with several openings. These 'tents', which should not be confused with the tent-like retreats suspended in the webs of certain sheet web builders such as *Cyrtophora* (see Chapter 5), are often found in corners in houses or under rocks and stones.

A typical tent-dwelling species is *Uroctea durandi*, a Mediterranean spider that lives in rocky places. The retreat of *Uroctea* incorporates a feature that occurs elsewhere among other tent builders as well as some tube dwellers, as we have seen – signal or tripping lines radiating from the main entrance to the retreat that serve to alert the occupant to the presence of its prey.

Interestingly, *Uroctea* and some other tent-builders like the much smaller *Oecobius*, throw strong bands of silk around the prey, completely wrapping it before carrying it back to the retreat to be eaten. This behaviour, and the radiating strands of the web, give weight to the idea that the orb weavers described in Chapter 6 have evolved from spiders like these.

SHEET
AND
TANGLE

'. . . the newest houses, the first day they are
whited, will have both Spiders and Cobwebs
in them'.

Rev. E. Topsell, 1607 (after T. Mouffet)

Although the term 'spider's web' normally brings
to mind the familiar circular 'orb' construction,
there are many species that build webs of different
types. Some of these have a random tangled
appearance, while others take the form of a
smooth sheet of silken strands, and a few species
make webs that combine both of these designs.
Certain spiders live permanently on their sheets,
but many spend the day in tubular retreats attached to their webs; one of the best-known of
these is *Tegenaria*, the European House Spider,
whose 'home' we find in dark corners of rooms.

Because house spiders are so large and so
recognisable, numerous stories have been told
about encounters with them. On a number of
occasions I have heard of 'pets' (with names like
Sidney or Sam) emerging from below the family
sofa every evening, apparently to watch television.
In fact, their transparent sheet web will have been
made on the carpet and the near-blind spider
comes to wait for prey, oblivious of the giants
around him – and the entertainment!

*Summoned by their mother with a tug on her
tangled web, immature Theridion sisyphium
spiders feed on a hoverfly she has killed*

Above: *modern, centrally-heated homes are too dry to be ideally suited to* Tegenaria gigantea. *Here a thirsty specimen takes a drink*

Above: *the extensive sheet web and superstructure built by* Agelena labyrinthica *in low bushes is a perfect trap for grasshoppers*

Struggle to the end

A genus closely related to the House Spiders, *Agelena*, gives its name to the family that contains them both – the *Agelenidae*. The web of *A. labyrinthica* has a much larger sheet than that of its domestic cousins, and this is held in place by an extensive superstructure of tangled lines above it. This also functions as a trap for low-flying or leaping insects, which are caught in mid-flight and drop on to the sheet.

Imagine a grasshopper, for example, falling on the sheet, its legs poking through the fine holes. It attempts to leap to safety but because of its uncertain foothold cannot jump with much force; it hits the tangled skein above the web and lands back on the sheet. Once the grasshopper is exhausted by its struggles, the spider runs effortlessly across the web and gives the unfortunate creature a nip on one of its legs. It backs off and then repeatedly attacks from different angles, rather like a dog would. Once the poison has begun to take effect and the grasshopper's movements have subsided, the spider grips it in its fangs, pulls it back to the mouth of its tube and begins to enjoy its meal.

Agelenids have a world-wide distribution, represented in North America by *Agelenopsis* and several other species in closely related genera. The majority of this family are found in the northern hemisphere, but Australia has *Corasoides*, which makes similar webs to *Agelena*, and occurs in the same habitats – low bushes and grassy plots. In New Zealand the allied genus *Cambridgea* was once classed with the agelenids but is now grouped with the *Stiphidiidae*. A common species on the South Island, *C. antipodiana*, is a large long-legged spider that wanders into houses, its size and habits no doubt explaining why it was formerly classified with the European House Spiders. This species also makes a sheet web, with a system of guy ropes above and below it that is reminiscent of the handywork of the very much smaller linyphiids (or money spiders), which are found mainly in the temperate parts of the northern hemisphere. By no means all of them make webs but the most conspicuous are those that make guyed sheets (like *Agelena*) but without the tubular retreat. Like *Cambridgea*, the linyphiids hang underneath the web and wait for prey to bump into the upper guy lines and fall on to the sheet. Then they run along below the web and bite their victims' legs as these protrude through the sheet, quickly paralysing the prey and dragging it through the silken membrane. *Linyphia triangularis* is the most numerous species of the family and probably the most common British spider. It is remarkably catholic in its choice of web sites, these ranging from ground level to several metres up and occurring in all types of habitat from open wind-swept heaths to the dark interiors of forests. From their very numbers it is safe to assume that they take a severe toll of insects in the summer and autumn.

Left: *an intruding spider like this immature hunter* Pisaura mirabilis *is just as helpless on the convex sheet web of* Linyphia triangularis *as any insect – and as quickly caught*

Below: *like many linyphiids,* L. montana *makes a sheet web with strands above it to strengthen the structure and entangle insects. When the prey drops on to the sheet, the spider attacks it from below, pulling it into the sheet as it is bitten and paralysed, then devoured*

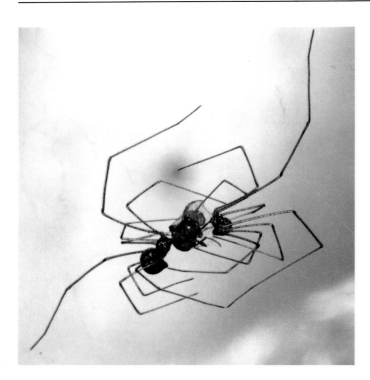

Above: *the typically long legs of these* Pholcus *spiderlings appear in danger of becoming permanently entangled as they share their prey*

Several members of the family make an extra sheet below the main one, the purpose of which seems to be the protection of the spider as it hangs in wait. Even some of the tiniest species, whose webs may be in a curled leaf lying on a woodland floor, put such a barrier web between themselves and the bottom of the leaf.

A silken trap

The pholcids are a family of spiders that have no separate sheet webs, but only a tangle of lines (some of them do, however, develop a small sheet or dome of silk within the tangle). *Pholcus phalangioides*, long in leg as well as name, is a house-dwelling species of the northern hemisphere, although found as well in rock crannies and caves in the warmer parts of its range. *Pholcus* has a fragile appearance, with a cylindrical abdomen and enormously long legs, and its web consists of widely-spaced strands, scattered apparently at random. The spider skulks at the top of the structure, in the darkest corner of the web, and in the evening it descends to the middle of its tangle and waits, in the typical inverted posture of the aerial weavers. If the web is touched and the spider knows that the vibrations in the strands are not caused by prey, it starts to gyrate its body at great speed as it retreats to the innermost part of its silky

labyrinth; this alarming-looking behaviour is presumably an attempt to dislodge or frighten off the intruder.

These spiders have a wide range of prey, including moths, woodlice, and other spiders and when the prey gets entangled, *Pholcus* comes bounding along to it and then turns its back. Just as you are wondering whether this is a sign of rejection, you see the long legs throwing fine strands around the prey. This continues until the latter is well and truly enswathed, then the package is held with the claws on the spider's back legs and dragged off into the depths of the web, where it is devoured. *Pholcus* has small chelicerae, capable of very little movement, and the spider has to probe its parcel to find a thin extremity it can stab.

Lines of death

The *Theridiidae* are a world-wide family with many species, whose webs, like that of *Pholcus*, are three-dimensional tangles. *Theridion*, from which the family takes its name, has more species than any other genus, each of them small, with a glossy appearance and attractive colours and patterns. Some of these are found frequenting houses but most sling their webs on low plants and bushes. Unlike *Pholcus*, most of them make a small cup-shaped retreat where they live in the daytime, although like most spiders they come out on to the web at dusk. They will feed by night or day, snaring their prey on strands coated with a sticky secretion that holds the victim until the spider arrives. Like *Pholcus* and other aerial-web makers they turn their backs on their prey to wrap it securely in silk before taking it back to the retreat for consumption.

In America and Australia another theridiid – *Steatoda* – has become a common house-dweller. This is a distinctive genus of brownish spiders with a white band across the abdomen. Larger than most other theridiids and longer-lived than the majority of web-builders, they make a flat, horizontal sheet in the middle of their tangle webs. Those species living near ground level place taut silk lines running down from the sheet; these lines have globules of adhesive near the bottom and a weak link where the lines actually touch the ground. When an ant or beetle gets accidentally stuck on one of these sticky feet it starts to struggle and pull itself free. Suddenly the line breaks at the weakest point and hoists the insect up into the air where its wriggling brings it into contact with more of the glue. The spiders often have tubular retreats

Left: Theridion sisyphium, *a common spider in Europe, is one of several retreat builders that indulge in the particularly gruesome practice of fixing the cadavers of their victims to the outside of their shelters*

Below left: *a beetle* (Lagria hirta) *is killed and wrapped before being eaten by* Steatoda bipunctata *even though this insect, in common with many others, tries to deter potential predators by exuding a foul liquid from its joints*

Bottom left: *the tough silk retreat of the southern European 'Black Widow',* Latrodectus tredecimguttatus *reveals what a formidable spider it is. Attached to it are the empty husks of several beetles, all over 30mm in length; the spider is only half as long*

(like the agelenids) and come dashing out to haul in their catch, which, in common with all theridiids, they wrap in sticky silk – moderate amounts for smaller prey or large drops thrown on potentially dangerous insects.

Killers in black

The Black Widow spider *Latrodectus mactans* from the USA is also a theridiid and is one of the best known of the sheet-web builders. On numerous occasions it has inflicted painful bites, sometimes resulting in the death of its human victim, although the incidence of fatalities may formerly have been increased by the use of inappropriate antidotes.

The Widows are the largest of the theridiids at a maximum body length of 16mm, but a much smaller spider with a similar appearance – *Dipoena* – terrorizes even the most aggressive insects to be found in northern Europe. *D. tristis* is only a quarter of the length of *Latrodectus* and much smaller than its own prey, the Wood Ant *Formica rufa*; if this ferocious creature tumbles into the web of the diminutive *Dipoena* it is as good as dead. Sticky silk is thrown by the spider, which stays well clear of the ant's formidable jaws, and then a small bite is made in one of *Formica's* legs and the poison quickly takes effect. The ant's violent struggles soon cease and the spider seizes a leg and proceeds to reduce its victim to an empty husk. Most surprisingly, the spider can tolerate the ant's formic acid, the fumes from which can even kill the ant itself if it is kept in a confined space for a short while.

Above: *tiny but fierce*, Dipoena tristis *uses its potent venom to paralyse the much larger and equally aggressive European wood ant* Formica rufa *that has fallen into its web*

Diving bell

One of the most curious of the tangle-web weavers is *Argyroneta* – the water spider. It is unique in its habitat, being the only spider to live permanently under water, through which it swims gracefully, clothed in a silvery bubble of air that allows it to breathe in the same way as other spiders. The lines of its 'web' are attached to aquatic plants and keep its submarine retreat securely in place: this retreat is an inverted silken cup filled with air brought from the surface by the spider. In common with terrestrial species the water spider can only feed in air so the little aquatic creatures on which it feeds must be taken back to the bell before the meal can start. During the winter months it spends its time sealed in this bell, which is given extra layers of silk to prevent the air from escaping.

Fatal vision

A family of spiders that makes a strange and specialized use of its tangle web is *Dinopidae*. They have been given several common names – Ogre-faced, Retiarus or Net-casting spiders. The first rather unkindly refers to their enormous eyes and the last two names show that they make the most extraordinary web, and they use it in a way that could be out of science fiction.

The lanky spider flattens its body against a twig during the day and is perfectly camouflaged, but when night comes it begins to make a tangle of elastic threads below its perch. It orientates itself head upwards and, within a square framework of silk the size of a postage stamp, cards a series of cribellate strands across this frame. The spider then reverses its position and grips the four corners of the tiny sheet with its front legs, stretching it a few times as if testing its strength. When this is done, the spider waits. Although it is dark, the huge eyes can detect the slightest movement and when a beetle scurries below, the spider lunges down toward it, still holding the net, then scoops up the unfortunate creature in the sticky trap. A few more jerks by the spider and the beetle is completely entangled, wrapped for good measure, and eaten. This net-casting spider is unique in that while it is feeding it can begin to construct a new trap – the food is handled only by the palps.

Left: *the infamous 'Black Widow' of the USA,* Latrodectus mactans, *one of the few spiders that is dangerous to man. Early reports of spider-related deaths however, may have been increased by the many inappropriate cures administered*

Top: *fringes of hair below the legs (which may act as paddles) are all that distinguish* Argyroneta aquatica *from many land-based spiders*

Above: *with the onset of cold weather, A. aquatica adds extra layers of silk to its bell, making it perfectly air tight*

Left: Dinopis stauntoni *hangs face down with the net held between its legs, ready to drop it over any small insect passing below*

THE ORB WEAVERS

'The spider as an artist has never been employed,
Though his surpassing merit is freely certified.'

Emily Dickinson (c. 1873)

To the casual observer, the orb-web weavers might seem to represent almost the whole order of spiders, and because of their abundance and high visibility, more is known about their biology and ecology than any other comparable group. The typical orb web must be renewed daily, so there are plenty of opportunities to watch the complex process taking place, though it all happens so quickly that it is easy for the observer to overlook the finer points. Although closely related orb-weaving species make webs that are similar, the snares of many others are highly individual and an absent owner can often be identified solely by his handiwork. The webs can be found in almost every kind of habitat but the vast majority are stretched on bushes or strung between them.

Silken strength
It was the sight of a garden spider, *Araneus diadematus*, that first stimulated my own interest in spiders. The web of this species is very large compared with the size of the spider itself: an

Orb webs are complex and beautiful feats of engineering. The builder of this one is a European garden spider – Araneus diadematus

individual 18mm in body length can make a web 500mm in diameter, using up to 20 metres of silk line. Because of the fineness of the silk, the web is extremely light and the spider itself can be a thousand times as heavy as its own web. Not only does this structure support the spider – at rest and in motion – it is also capable of trapping strong, fast-flying insects.

Some of the largest and heaviest spiders (apart from the mygalomorphs) are found among the orb-web weavers. The heaviest European spider, for example, is another species of *Araneus* – *A. quadratus*. This is a large rotund species, normally reaching up to 15mm in body length, but in 1979 there was found on a heath in southern England a female 20mm long, weighing 2.25g. This giantess weighed four thousand times as much as her web!

A number of spiders in the genera *Cyclosa*, *Argiope* and *Uloborus* add dense ribbons of silk (known as *stabilmenta*) to their webs, and these appear to have a variety of functions. In some species they may be used to strengthen and stabilize the web (hence their name) but in the case of *Cyclosa* and *Uloborus* (spiders that live permanently on the hubs of their webs) they evidently serve as camouflage, since they blend perfectly

with the spiders' own patterning. These bands may also be used as moulting platforms or as shade from the sun and the cosmopolitan genus *Argiope* produces very showy stabilmenta designed to frighten off the birds or at least to deter them from flying through the webs. Most *Argiope* species are striped in yellow, white and black, a pattern that is common among arthropods and means 'Don't eat me – I taste unpleasant', and the banded stabilmenta of these spiders reinforce the message. Some orb-web weavers spend their whole lives sitting out on the hubs of their webs and making frequent forays to gather insects that blunder into them. Others silk together leaves to form a retreat, which is linked to the hub by silken lines that convey the vibrations of a struggling insect back to the spider. These retreats are normally hidden in

Top: *orb weavers know their craft from birth. Here, a young* Araneus diadematus *has built a web even more symmetrical than an adult's*

Right: *in a web it has adorned with warning flags of silk, the brightly-striped* Argiope bruennichi *spider sends a clear message to all potential predators – keep off!*

Above: *another spider that makes a stabilmentum is* Uloborus walckenaerius, *a cribellate species whose durable horizontal webs are not viscid*

Above: Cyclosa conica *from northern Europe builds a conspicuous vertical stabilmentum across the hub of its web*

nearby vegetation but a few species, such as *Metepeira labyrinthica*, build them in the webs themselves. (*Metepeira* also adds the protection of a tangle-web barrier to its web-based retreat).

A perilous flight

As might be expected, the great number of species of orb-web weavers has led to an extensive variety of web forms and modifications to the basic orb shape. Yet two spiders from opposite sides of the globe have evolved fascinatingly similar adaptations to deal with the same problem – catching the moths on which it lives.

Most moths are nocturnal and have developed various strategies to avoid night-active predators. As far as the sticky webs of the orb weavers are concerned, moths rely on the scales that cover their wings. When the moth touches a web the scales adhere, but they are easily shed, rendering the insect virtually 'non-stick'. A New Guinea spider, *Tylorida*, makes its orb web in the conventional way but in an extremely elongated shape, with the hub near the top. The upper radii are very short and the lower ones, forming in effect a ladder (the 'rungs' being the nearly horizontal sections of the spiral) are greatly lengthened (fig. 000). When a moth hits the web it falls down the ladder, progressively losing scales as it goes, until at last it is 'bald' and sticks to the web, where the spider can attack it. A Colombian Ladder Spider uses a very similar technique but in this case the hub is near the bottom of the web and the ladder stretches upwards from it.

Another New Guinea species, *Pasilobus*, uses a variant of the ladder principle to overcome the defences of the moths on which it feeds. The web has only three radii, which are strung out horizontally, and the 'hub' is merely the convergence point of the radii; the two dry lines that cross the web near this point form the spider's retreat. The viscid catching spiral in this case has been reduced to a dozen or so bridging threads sagging below the radii and loaded with gluey blobs. The spider waits in its retreat for the first moth of the night to fly into one of the sticky loops and become hopelessly entangled. It then dashes to the attack, biting and wrapping its prey before carrying it back to the retreat to be eaten.

Two more orb weavers specialize in moths – *Mastophora* in the Americas and *Dicrostichus* from Australia – but these two spiders have reduced their webs to a single line and each preys exclusively on one or two local species of moth, and

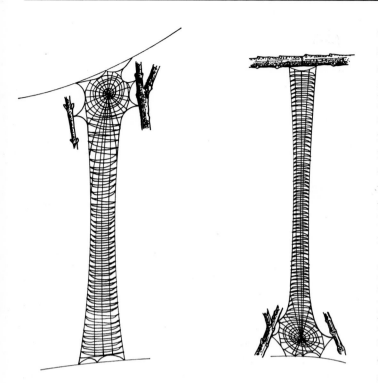

Above: *two spiders from opposite ends of the globe have evolved strangely similar methods for catching moths. By shedding wing-scales, moths often evade capture, but one species from New Guinea and another from Colombia get round this by building ladder-like extensions to their webs. In each case the moth tumbles down the 'rungs' and runs out of scales, but while the former ladder is below the hub of its web, the latter one is above it. The end result is the same however for the doomed moth*

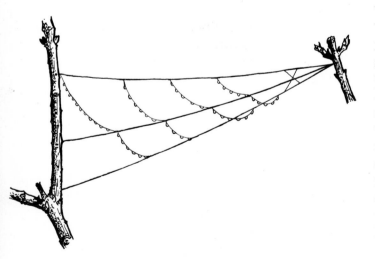

Above: Pasilobus, *also from New Guinea, has further refined the orb web. Making only three radii, the spider adds sticky cross-lines, each with a weak 'link'. When a moth hits a line the thread breaks at one end, the prey is left hanging and is soon caught by the spider*

then only the male insects. The spider makes a short thread covered with sticky material and then combs this glue down until a large blob is formed at the end of the thread – the bolas is ready. Experiments have shown that these spiders are able to mimic the sex pheromones (signal scent) of female moths and as the male insect approaches from down wind the spider detects the fluttering of his wings and starts swinging the sticky bolas – the hapless moth flies to its destruction. *Celaenia*, the Australian Orchard Spider, uses the same lure but merely dangles on a thread and grabs the moths as they fly in.

Ingenious constructions

One of the most eccentric of orb weavers is the rare *Paraplectanoides crassipes*, found in Tasmania and New South Wales. The 'barrier' web of this species consists of a thick wall in a shape reminiscent of a deflated football, which completely surrounds the orb web. The orb itself is much simplified, consisting solely of a thickened hub, connected to the outer wall by radiating lines, and a small hole is left in the barrier to arouse the curiosity of the springtails and cockroaches upon which the spider feeds. Once the insect is inside the ball, its movements are communicated by the radii to the waiting spider, which rushes along the nearest line to capture the prey and carry it back to the hub to be eaten.

Spiders of the genus *Hyptiotes* also make a web unlike any other. This is a mere slice of the normal web, not unlike that of *Pasilobus*, but strung vertically and made of dry silk. Four radii are joined by cribellate links, and the point of convergence of the radii is extended backwards in a single thread to the spider, which grips it with its front legs. The spider's rear legs hang on to a short strand of silk that anchors it to the branch of the tree in which it builds its web, and thus the spider itself makes a bridge. When prey hits the web, the spider's spinners let out silk, and the spider shoots forward so that the catching web partly collapses, entangling the prey in more lines. This continues until the spider reaches its victim and wraps it for later consumption.

Overleaf: *the body of* Hyptiotes paradoxus *forms a bridge between its anchor line and the single thread running to its web – a much-reduced orb not unlike that of* Pasilobus, *but strung in a more vertical plane than that of the New Guinea species and with four radii rather than three*

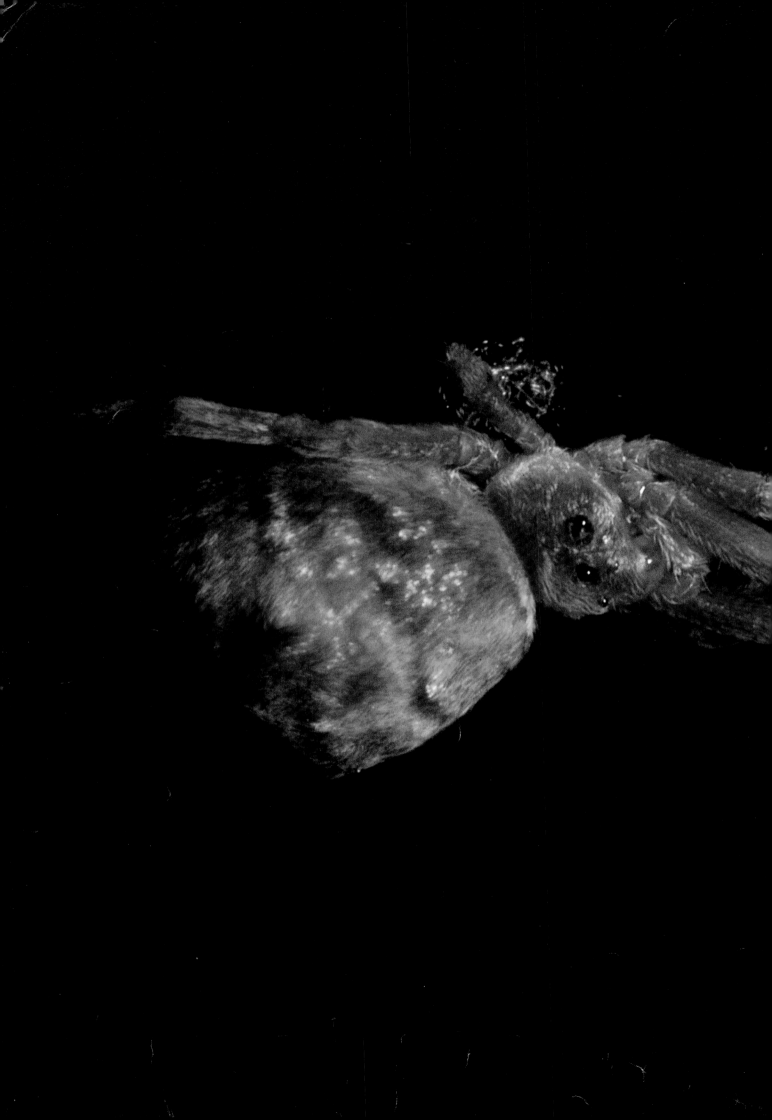

The orb web

The construction of this type of web, with its geometrical design, is a marvel of animal engineering that is accomplished within the space of half an hour. All of the steps in the process are instinctive and more or less unvarying; no use is made of vision, the spider employing only its delicate sense of touch to gauge the position and tension of the threads. The building of a web is often done at night, but if stormy weather prevents this the spider will build at the earliest opportunity, day or night.

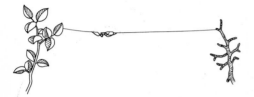

The bridge

The spider's first move is to secure a bridge line, from which the finished web will hang, by spinning a long strand of silk and allowing it to stream out in the air. When the thread gets snagged on some piece of vegetation, which may be some way off or even on the other side of running water, the spider pulls on the line to see if it will bear its weight and then reinforces it by laying further strands of silk along it.

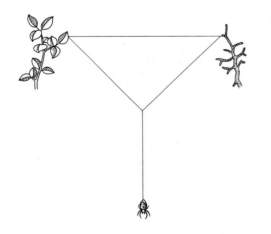

The Y-frame

Having made a suitably strong bridge line, the spider then runs along it, trailing a loose second line, which it fixes securely at each end of the bridge. Then it returns along this loose strand and spins a third thread vertically from its centre point. Pulling this third line down by its own weight the spider descends until it encounters a solid object,

to which it fixes the line. The spider has now established a basic framework in the shape of the letter Y – the centre of the Y will be the centre of the web.

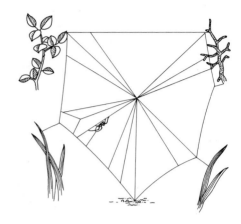

Frame lines and radii

The spider now returns to each end of the bridge and spins further frame lines, in which the web will ultimately be enclosed. By climbing along existing lines and trailing further lines behind, the spider then constructs more radii. Within a few minutes as many as 40 of these may be made, all carefully positioned to keep the tension in the web evenly balanced. Before the spider considers this phase to be complete it goes to the centre of the web and touches each radius in turn; any that are unsatisfactory are removed and repositioned. Tiny irregularities, quite undetectable to the human eye, are corrected at this stage.

The hub

The spider now rotates at the centre of the web, spinning a tight spiral of silk. This is the hub, a central platform that is complete when its diameter is somewhat larger than the spider's leg-span.

The temporary spiral

Leaving an open zone around the edge of the hub, the spider now begins to spin an outer, temporary spiral, working towards the edges of the web, and when this is complete it rests for a few minutes. The purpose of this temporary spiral is to stabilize the web during construction and to act as a series of 'stepping-stones' for the spider.

The permanent spiral

When the spider resumes work, the silk issuing from its spinners changes from the dry lines used during the previous ten minutes and now has a sticky coating. The spider retraces its steps along the temporary spiral, this time working its way from the outer edge towards the centre, oil on its feet preventing it from sticking to its own web. As it proceeds it spins a permanent spiral of sticky threads, much more closely set than the temporary one (which is progressively destroyed as the spider advances). This is achieved by holding the thread under its mouth parts and dissolving it with digestive juices. For about twenty minutes the spider painstakingly winds its way towards the centre of the web. Each sticky segment of the new spiral is cemented to a radial line, quickly stretched, then attached to the next radius, while the spider's legs are touching existing lines, enabling it to space the new segments.

Above: Nuctenea umbratica *builds mostly on dead trees and hides its flattened body in a crevice in the bark during the day*

Tidying up

When the spider reaches the gap round the hub it leaves off spinning the viscid spiral, returns to the hub and dissolves the untidy tangle of threads accumulated there. Most spiders immediately replace this with tidy threads but some leave a neat hole in the very centre of the web.

The majority of webs hang in a more or less vertical plane and when the web is complete the spider clings on to the lower side of the hub, settles itself in a comfortable position with its head downwards, draws in its legs and waits for a meal.

Renewal

A successful web is, of course, damaged by the impact and the struggles of the very prey it is designed to catch, and the coating also becomes less sticky in time. Consequently the spider must build a new web every day, using the existing bridge line. The spider consumes the old web first and tests have shown that up to 90% of the silk that is ingested finds its way into the new web so that very little of the spider's substance is wasted. If the web catches no prey, the spider will begin again elsewhere.

INTERACTIONS

'I think the family is the place where the most ridiculous and least respectable things in the world go on'.

Ugo Betti, *The Inquiry* (1944–5)

So far we have examined many of the curious behaviour patterns to be found in the spider world. We have looked at what spiders eat, how they catch their prey, and how they evade their enemies. Solitary creatures for the most part, some of their most interesting behaviour is shown in their relations with each other.

Curious courtship

The solitary habits and predatory instincts of spiders can combine to create a serious problem for the courting male and the males of some species have evolved ingenious ways to disarm the females, who might otherwise regard their potential mates as prey. Some male spiders announce their amorous intentions by plucking gently on the strands of the female's web, while others opt for bribery. The *Pisaura mirabilis* male, for instance, presents a courtship gift of paralysed and silk-wrapped prey to the female and copulates with her while she is busy eating her present, whereas the male of the Eurasian orb-web weaver *Meta*

Many spiders have developed advanced social techniques. Here, a male Pisaura mirabilis *offers a silk-wrapped insect to his mate*

Above: *when the* Pisaura *male's gift is accepted, the female starts to feed and her attention is distracted from the giver*

(Metellina) segmentata employs a rather less generous courtship technique. He waits at the side of the female's web until an insect blunders into it; as soon as one does so and the female has dashed across to bite and wrap it, he hurries to mate with her while her attention is temporarily distracted by her meal. The wait for an insect to turn up might be a long one, so that in the autumn dozens of anticipatory males can be seen on the outskirts of the web (the female on the hub) their reproductive fortunes hingeing precariously on the arrival of some luckless insect.

With the majority of orb weavers the male stays in the female's web for only an hour or so before taking his leave, but the males of numerous other web-making species spend most of their adult lives with their mates, enjoying, as we have seen, mainly good relations. Over the years I have kept various species of the European House Spider *Tegenaria* and they have rewarded me with some amusing

glimpses into their private lives. *T. gigantea* is, as its name suggests, a formidable-looking spider; the female is up to 18mm in body length, with legs twice as long. One pair I had quickly made themselves at home in an old shoe box containing a cardboard tube for them to hide in during the day. The box was soon filled with sheet web, and flies I tossed in were chased and killed. When there are two spiders after the same prey the nearer one usually gets it, but on one occasion I saw the female rudely push aside her mate and steal the fly he had just caught. I chose to believe that he was chivalrously allowing his egg-laden spouse to feed, but later, while observing another pair, I saw the male chase off the female from her prey and eat it himself – so much for chivalry!

The rarest British *Tegenaria* in houses, *T. parietina*, is a spider of even more imposing dimensions than my other house guests. The legs of the female are up to 50mm long, whilst those of the male can be 80mm. When a friend sent me a pair of these spiders I was delighted, and thinking that such a large species would need a sizeable prey I threw them a grasshopper. Instead of the lusty

Above: *the male's cunning strategy having paid off, he promptly seizes his opportunity to mate with the preoccupied female*

chase I had expected, the two spiders went into what I can only describe as a blind panic and headed for the safety of their retreat. Unfortunately they both arrived together and soon became hopelessly entangled, with spindly legs waving in all directions. I was convulsed with laughter and wondered how we humans could possibly fear such timid creatures.

Maternal care

Once spiders have mated and eggs have been laid, the newly-hatched spiderlings can exist for some time on the remains of the yolk, but eventually they must find some tiny prey to catch. In about twenty species, however, the young are provided with food by their mothers. In the case of the European agelenid *Coelotes terrestris*, the spiderlings remain in their mother's web for about a month and during this time she responds to their 'begging' by turning over softened prey to them.

The young of several species of theridiid are fed directly by their mother, chiefly on a regurgitated liquid that they cluster round her mouth to drink. After their first moult, the mother spider catches prey for them and calls the brood down from the retreat by tugging on the web strands. She can easily distinguish between vibrations caused by prey and the movements of her offspring. Even the spiderlings know the difference between calls to eat and alarm vibrations, the latter sending them scurrying to the retreat.

Spider societies

Thirteen species of spider have been found that are truly social, living peacefully in large groups of adults and juveniles and attacking prey co-operatively. In four species of the cribellate *Stegodyphus*, the spiderlings can approach any female in the group to be fed, while an allied species, *Dresserus armatus*, exhibits an even stranger example of social behaviour. The female lays several egg sacs and not only do the first brood scavenge on her remains when she is dead (as a few other spiders do) but they also give food to their more recently

Top: *like theridiid young who feed together, these newly-hatched spiderlings of* Argiope trifasciata *enjoy a communal drink from a raindrop adhering to the strands of silk they have spun*

hatched siblings, feeding their younger brothers and sisters for up to half an hour at a time.

The non-cribellate (ecribellate) species *Agelena republicana* and *Anelosimus eximius*, which weave sheet and tangle webs respectively, co-operate to construct a single giant web, much larger than any solitary spider could make. Hundreds of individuals live on the web and gang up on any large prey that lands on it.

The Paraguayan orb weaver *Eriophora bistriata* bridges the gap between solitary and social behaviour, living in colonies of up to 300 individuals, each building its own web on communally-spun support lines. Small prey is dealt with in the usual way but if it is too large to be tackled by a single spider it attracts the attention of neighbours, who leave their own webs and join in the capture and feeding of the victim.

Some of the *Cyrtophora* species build communal webs but there is no social co-operation here. The juveniles make their smaller webs in the rigging of those of the adult females, but if an unlucky youngster falls into its mother's web it will be seized and eaten! A number of web-building species make individual webs that are very close together but they also do not exhibit any predatory behaviour that can really be described as co-operative. The young common European orb weavers, *Nuctenea cornuta*, for example, sometimes use each other's frame threads, so that numerous webs are packed into a small space.

Intimate relationships

Among the theridiids is a parasitic genus – *Argyrodes* – with numerous species that live on the webs of host spiders and steal their prey: this behaviour is described as *kleptoparasitic*. An even more intimate relationship exists between another spider, *Curimagua bayano*, and its host, the very much larger *Diplura*. The tiny parasite rides, apparently unnoticed, on *Diplura*'s body and is able to climb down the chelicerae of its host and share in the 'soup'.

All spiders are predatory, and whilst most of their attention is fixed on insects, all of them indulge in eating their own kind. The habit of cannibalism may be encouraged by the sheer numbers of spiderlings produced from some egg-sacs; the weaker individuals are devoured by their more active siblings.

Most vagrant hunters can run away from each other if they meet but if a hunter falls into a web it is as helpless as any insect. Yet there is one family are *Mimetus* and the smaller *Ero*, both of whom stealthily invade the webs of other species and bite the luckless occupants. *Ero's* poison is very are *Mimetus* and the smaller *Ero*; the latter stealthily invades the webs of other species and bites the luckless occupants. *Ero's* poison is very fast-acting on the victim, and in a few seconds the Pirate Spider is feeding on its prey. *E. furcata* can even imitate the courting signals of a male *Meta (Metellina) segmentata* to lure the female.

An unfinished story
The story of the spider is stranger by far than the myth of Arachne, who gave her name to the order

Above: *the 'Pirate Spider' Ero tuberculata preys exclusively on other spiders. In this case a young theridiid (right) has fallen victim to the pirate's deadly poison*

of creatures we have been examining. Some 50,000 species from every part of the globe have been identified and described and almost certainly many more species and curious variations in behaviour are still waiting to be discovered. What is beyond doubt, however, is that these adaptable and versatile creatures will continue to exert their fascination on naturalists and laymen alike. We can love spiders or hate them, but once we have had a glimpse into their strange and secret lives we can never wholly ignore them again.

Overleaf: *during the autumn months, the male of the common European spider* Meta (Metellina) segmentata *waits patiently at the edge of the female's web until she approaches a trapped insect. When her energies are concentrated elsewhere, he dashes in to mate with her – a cunning ruse that ensures the survival of the species*

INDEX